my pen + paper = a poetry book©

by Elliot M. Rubin

Cover image by jessica45 from Pixabay

Copyright Library of Congress
May 2020

ISBN - 978-1-7328493-7-2

Dedication
To my grandchildren
Shane, Isabelle, Jonathan, Carter,
Alexandra, Melanie, Mollie, and Madison

In Memory of
Herman S. Rubin
Who wrote poetry all his life.

Preface

Poetry is to be read and understood. To be written in plain English for everyone's enjoyment. Too often, poets write in-depth, penetrating poems where you need to be well-read and versed in literature's nuances to appreciate the poetry, not this book or any of my writings.

Table of Contents

her love

she is named
after the full
celestial moon,
reflected light
touching lives below

as in the night
her aura
shines on all
infecting them
with a wide smile

love is transferable
between two people,
sometimes easy to find,
yet hard to keep if you
forget how you found it

her love is a jewel
to be taken to heart,
treasured as a valuable
object, kept alive
forever in your soul
for better or worse

understanding

i understand why some don't believe
in a deity, unseen, untouchable,
beyond logic to many- yet some do

i understand why people follow
despots, money to gain,
racial bias, many are gullible

what i don't understand is why educated
people don't believe in climate change,
when proven by scientific means

yet they believe in a deity,
follow an incompetent despot,
and trust everything he says

my head spins from illogical logic

a spring drive

at dawn this morning
as i drove
by the fresh-cut field,
the rising sun
burned the thin
layer of dew
off the grass,
permeating
the slightest breeze
with a sweet scent
of nature,
causing it to
waft into
my deepest memories
as a five-year-old;
climbing through
the barbwire fence
on the farm one summer
with my cousin;
to begin our day's adventure
in the cow pasture
trying to avoid
the minefield of manure
saturated with flies,
as the cows in the distance
watch us,
with disdain
in their eyes

depression

the blackness
is descending,
i'm surrounded
by plague,
death is everywhere

only sequestered
in my self-made prison
do i feel secure
until supplies
start to dissipate
forcing me
to venture out

people i know
have succumbed,
some older,
some younger

lives needlessly lost.
how do i go on,
how do i make sense
of this chaos?

i don't know,
except to open my eyes
in the morning
then step out of bed,
breathing in,
then exhaling,
while thanking
a higher power
for another day
i wait out

the darkness
expecting tomorrow
to see the light
at the end
of this nightmare

prayer

i remember the day well
when i realized
i was not
getting anything
out of the religious service

it was about
the middle
when i stood
then walked out-
it has been
at least ten years
if not more
since i've been back

in biblical times
there were no
organized prayers books
people recited by rote
from their mouth
not from their soul-

their heart
spoke to god,
not from
someone else's
words in a book

together forever

the wedding ceremony
was beautiful-
dressed in white,
flowers in bloom everywhere
they walked down the aisle
hand in hand
ready to start
a life together
forever

in the judge's office
the divorce ceremony
is different.
drab and official
walnut paneling
on the walls
it is cut and dry,
with the signing of papers
never-ending

afterward
they walk
out clutching
in both their hands
the final decree,
knowing
it will be
forever

the carnival

years ago a carnival
came to town one week
with games of chance,
trying to win a doll
for my girlfriend,
or the red plastic dice
on a string
to hang
over my inside
car mirror

the rides are fun too-
sitting next to her
gravity pushes
us closer
until we almost merged
together

marriage is like the carnival-
many memories,
many mementos and
many times together

remember
all rides
have a start and finish,
her passing
will end a great ride

death 2020

the hallways of death are full
of bodies lined up waiting,
waiting to be cremated
because the morgue is full,
refrigerated trailers are full,
funeral homes are full,
doctor's lounges are full,
the pediatric floor is full
of adults dying,
the kids moved to other hospitals-

my daughter works in
the hallways of death

the president is also full
of self-import
with no empathy,
unless it is written
on the notes
he listlessly reads
robotically

the wedding incident

it was a big wedding
lots of food and drink for all
as she floated in the room
greeting everyone with a smile
and a kiss on the cheek,
all the guests turn to say hello
until she stops in front of me-
her husband stands behind
when he turns to greet friends
while she places her hand on
the nap of my neck, pulling
me in, planting her lips on mine-
we never dated but met a few times
before, years ago, in social gatherings

her long blond hair drapes
on her shoulder as her other hand
softly touches my cheek

i could taste the whiskey
on her tongue as it swirls in
my mouth; while she ignores my
wife sitting only feet away

the band starts to play when
her husband turns to dance
enabling me to sit at my table;
wondering what her next move
will be-
later she came to ask for my
phone number, i gave her
a wrong one-
living in another state
i knew i was safe.

my wife asks why she wants
the cell number;
i answer her honestly...
i'm eye candy
luckily, she has a sense of humor

an evening in New Orleans

after sundown the music
is blaring from the open
doors of the bars lining
Bourbon Street as i try to walk
through the mass of bodies
jammed together while i soak
up the smell and atmosphere
of New Orleans at party time

filigree iron railings on the second
story of the buildings reflect
the elegance in the French Quarter;
while women below stagger
out of bars exposing themselves
to men passing by,
inebriated, too drunk to take
advantage of the situation

when i see men and women
stagger down the street
i think of the thousands of
generations that preceded us,
outliving the perils of life
only to end up on the
asphalt gutter, prone, arrested
and carted off for the evening

sleep

years ago, i did not sleep well-
i woke to go to work early
one morning, had breakfast,
then opened the medical vials
and took my morning meds

started the car and drove off-
by the time i reached two blocks
i really felt tired,
very tired,
incredibly tired

so i parked the car, closed my eyes
then eight hours later, i wake up-
i realize how long i slept.
i had opened one of my wife's vials,
it was her sleeping pills

the moral of this story
is to keep your pills separate-
chalk this episode up to
just another life experience
on the path of life

the single tree

is she a leftover lover while he is locked in,
separated from her until they can be
together again,

loneliness and boredom cause him
to search online for someone else
to talk with, tease with, flirt with,
maybe make plans with

will he still want her once free to roam
amongst the trees in the forest of singles?

he forgets she can do the same thing.
maybe she wants more than he can give her,
in more ways than one

she has value to give as she sees fit,
not put in his back pocket brought
out when wants-
her tree in the forest is tall and robust,
roots soaking up mother earth's nutrients
making her fearless and brave,
wanting to desire on her terms,
not needing to be wanted on his

the question

they dated for a while
when he decides to
pop the question

will you marry me?
i want an old fashion
marriage, like in the bible;
where you tend the house,
raise our kids and take care of
any dogs or animals we have

so i'm to give up my career,
pop out babies for you,
not use the education i earned,
and take care of any animals?

yes

i'll tell you how i'm going
to take care of the animals;
i'm letting one animal
out of the gate right now

goodbye jackass

the mask

she was full of bravado and energy
forging forward every day
in a profession she's forced into,
to live day-to-day to survive

she carries a switchblade in
a coat pocket for protection;
johns can be dangerous, especially
when they refuse to pay her afterward

tough as nails, she does what she
needs to do. in early morning hours,
a car service brings her to a
third-floor walk-up apartment

after a shower, she slouches naked
on the sofa, fluffs a pillow to relax
with a cold beer, and thinks back
to her sweet innocent childhood

removing her mask of invincibility

a ticked off poem

a weak president
with a weak mind
who thinks he's strong
is so very wrong

he foments revolt
cause he's a dolt
supporting gun rights
with kids in their sights

the states need a test
he proclaims he's the best
his brain's better than the rest
truth is, he is full of bull shit
[sorry it did not rhyme]

so stay inside
time will abide
start to create
wait for a date
when we can
go outside

stay safe

heaven

i'm not waiting for heaven-
an amorphous unknown
when here and now
i can see beauty,
i can touch beauty,
i can feel the beauty
with my heart,
with my hands,
with my fingers,
and my lips

i choose to live
for now,
in a life
full of beauty
all around me

instead of waiting
for something
no one knows exists,
except for tales
from the past,
kept alive
by word of mouth
with no proof,
just faith-
i'm not waiting for heaven

May-December lovers

i'm looking down
at my hands,
blue veins popping up
under weathered wrinkles
of aged skin
showing the years
of a life's experiences

glancing over
to her young hands,
the smooth skin
so supple to the touch
without a blemish,
scar, callous free,
nails so pink
they tell of a life
not yet lived

holding her body
now close to mine
reminds me
of melting butter,
waiting to be spread
on soft, fresh bread
with a smooth, tender touch,
to be tasted-
savored
by an old man
on his last hurrah

East 21 Street, Brooklyn

it is lonely
being a survivor
going back to the street i grew up on
one last time, as an old man-
i stand on the sewer cover
my friends and i used as home plate
playing punchball till dusk,
until we couldn't see
the pink rubber ball anymore-
i see them by the old buick (first base)
running to the next sewer cover
to get the ball;
we had no need for other bases,
the eight of us guys, now disbanded
after college, most dead, played all day long

i look at the victorian era homes
we all lived in, empty now of the people i knew
most of them now dead;
who live on only in my mind

depressed, i drive to my old elementary school
where we had air raid drills hiding under wooden
desks-
i remember my teachers,
the third-grade girl i fooled around with,
the long walks home after classes,
the assemblies with the whole school attending,
now all long gone;
the sidewalks are empty, quiet, no swarm of kids

i sit in my car to drive home,
leaving my memories, along with my tears,
on my old street

what a difference a month makes

i counted the months
i counted the weeks
i counted the days

it all started with the minutes
then grew until the time seemed so endless

finally, the day arrived-
my daughter is here
nine months later

1953 black & white photograph

standing on the sidewalk
in front of their furniture store
i see my father and uncle
brothers and partners
with the sun beating down on them
in their short sleeve shirts
pants pulled up high past their waists
with boxes of unopened furniture behind them
after the delivery truck left them there

the forty-foot sign on the front of the store
directly over their heads
shouts out the company name
to passerby's on coney island avenue
on a warm summer's day-
this was one of the good old days

a get together with friends

its midnight now
and they are all visiting me-
we reminisce about the days
playing ball together,
the double dates we went on,
the teachers we had in school,
the young student female teacher
who flirted with us-
exhausted from talking
i bid them goodnight
then fall back to sleep

high school homeroom

i remember Wendy O'Brian
a tall, lanky, Irish brunette
in my homeroom class-
i was smitten with her
but she only dated seniors
while i was a lowly freshman,
still too young for her desires-
yet decades later
i always remember her face,
her smile,
her walking into the room
every morning that year
wishing i was in her arms

some memories,
unlike people,
never die

a note to myself years later

you will have conquests
much prettier than most,
a beauty pageant winner
her picture in national magazines,
alas not a lasting love

but the beauty of the heart
is permanent,
not fleeting
like superficial things do

kindness, caring, and true love
will find you-
it will last decades
making many new memories

walk'n and talk'n with Jesus

as i walk down the staircase of life
i'm coming to the final few steps
where i'll end my long tiresome journey;
depression and despair are constant companions
when i hear a gentle voice whispering out to me;
wait and listen, so i did

come walk with me we'll talk a little-
he held my hand i felt so secure;
he gave me the hope i lost long ago;
i listened to words i forgot from my youth

i turned around and walked back up-
he was with me step by step,
never leaving me alone to fall

i walked and talked
with him a while;
i'm so glad;
i found a way
back home

8 o'clock

it's 8 o'clock, we finished dinner
on the cruise ship, then begin
the walk to the theater in the bow
for tonight's spectacular musical

walking our way through the bar
we pass a beautiful young blonde woman
in a form-fitting evening dress slouched
back in a club chair, passed out from drinks

standing next to her, seeming perplexed,
i assume is her husband or boyfriend asking
for help to get her back to their stateroom.
behind him is a young child looking bewildered

looking forward to a happy evening i
suddenly felt depressed and saddened-
embarrassed for the child to have strangers
stare at her mom with great pity in their eyes

self

who are you? i ask myself

it, i think, depends on my age at the time

in my preteen years, i was an innocent child,
dependent on my parents

in my teen years, i saw myself
absorbed in composing music,
and chasing big breasted,
small-breasted
and basically
any size bra-wearing
teenage girls

my adult self is married
and raising children-
too busy with business
too tired to create, just procreate

my senior years i am just creating,
letting my mindset the pace,
to leave in poetry
who I was,
and have become

vows

she walks down the aisle in love
with the thought of being married

yet as the vows are being said
she longs for her lover

"after obeying" is mentioned
she did not know what the vows
are for; as she has no intention
of being in a monogamous
marriage, and he did

lust for her lover is on her mind

the vows though,
 to her now-husband
are intended for him to keep,
not her

surprised

what do I tell her?
i never heard her speak
yet i hear her voice in her writing;
i feel as though we speak
the same language

today she wrote
saying the poems
she created
for the past three months
are new to her-
she never wrote
poetry before

erotic poems
never crossing the line
to obscenity,
yet arousing,
sensually done
but in good taste

i am surprised-
haven't answered
her back as of yet
don't know how to respond,
i am silent

Sadie

surrounded by four walls
plus a small plastic gate
she leads a solitary life
while my daughter is at work

when i visit
i need to call ahead
so Sadie is on a leash
and outside

visitors excite her-
best she's on the lawn
when i come to see them

i was the one who held her
in my arms next to my chest
when the selection to buy her
was made

nuzzling her soft furry head
under my neck,
rubbing it back and forth
while i hold her 20 pounds
of love in my arms

if only people would love
as unrestrained as she does

feelings of depression

the blackness is descending,
i'm surrounded by plague
death is everywhere i look-
only sequestered in my self
made prison do i feel secure,
until supplies start to dissipate
forcing me to venture out

people i know have succumbed;
some older some younger
lives needlessly lost-
how do i go on?
how do i make sense of this chaos?
i do not know except to open my eyes
in the morning and step out of bed,
breathing in, then exhaling, while thanking
a higher power for another day-
you wait out the darkness
expecting tomorrow
to see the light
at the end of this nightmare

understand logic

i understand
why some people
don't believe in a deity,
unseen,
untouchable,
beyond logic to many,
yet some do

i understand
why people follow
despots,
money to gain,
racial bias,
many are gullible

what I don't understand
is why educated people
don't believe in climate change,
when proven by scientific means

yet they believe in a deity,
follow an incompetent despot,
believing everything he says

my head spins
from illogical logic

a live diamond

she is standing
in front of you
with no clothes on,
yet you don't see her

all you can view
is your unbridled lust,
missing her desires,
her wants, her needs

after you finish,
walk out satisfied
you thoughtlessly
leave behind
an unpolished jewel

thinking a good
blind date ended-
but her value is her
kind heart, and
caring nature
you will never
get to see,
because she'll find
another date
who appreciates
the value
of hard to find gems

too much, too late, too often?

it's 8 o'clock, we finished dinner
on the cruise ship then begin the walk
to the theater in the bow of the ship
for tonight's spectacular musical

walking our way through the bar
we pass a beautiful young blonde
in a form-fitting black evening dress,
slouched back in a club chair
passed out from drinks

standing next to her looking perplexed,
is her husband asking for help
to get her back to their stateroom-
behind him, a young girl seems bewildered

looking forward to a happy evening
I suddenly felt empathy, then depression,
embarrassed for the child to have strangers
stare at her mother with disgust in their eyes

a farmer's pasture

i pass the fallow field
ablaze with yellow
dandelion buds
blooming from above
the green grass
blanket below

at a distance everything
seems pretty and bright

this reminds me
of some beautiful people
glamorous and opulent;
until i get closer
to the field-
i then realize
first impressions fade
when you see
plenty of weeds
in the field
of humanity

an adult blue poem of gibberish

the yellow phlip-ster only eats blue turnips
when it awakes from its winter slumber-
because the purple ones aren't in season;
that my friends are not the only reason,
the blue ones are favored
by the glum-ber too!
who sniffs out purple ones first
before anyone else, to eat purple them
before it sleeps

gustav the doorman goes to market
to buy blue turnips for the tenants,
especially purple ones if he can find them;
they are as rare as clean air

he tries to help miss zas-tov
who loves them too,
and always cries if she doesn't
eat them blue-
after eating a bushel or two
they both turn bright blue,
they eat them together
no matter the weather-
the moral of the story is
if you eat blue turnips
with your girlfriend,
you'll get blued!

blind love

he is kind, caring and gentle,
dresses nicely, not a showboat
has a well-paying job he has held
for many years plus a small house
on a hill overlooking the city, but single

she is beautiful and knows it
but is still single due to her
being picky about a man's looks-
she knows him they are friends

if he is slim, not overweight,
had a full head of hair,
more handsome face
she would be thrilled to date him-
if only love was blind

annoyed

my window is open
spring has arrived
the sweet scent
of early morning dew
being burnt off
by the sun
lulls me to nap

until the boy next door
starts his mower's engine

spring 1

spring is here
lots to do
there's a list-
i lost my spring

too many years
under my belt,
too many steps
on my feet

my spring is sprung,
strung out years ago-
i don't want
to get out of bed

spring 2

the light pink petals
on the barbed
rosebush, open
with the warmth
of the morning sun-
kissed so lightly
by a pollinating bee
with an exposed stinger,
reminds me of her
luscious lips,
prickly attitude,
and stinging wit

glad i survived

daisy in spring 3

the soft flutter
of bright yellow petals
swaying in the mild breeze,
on a tall,
thin,
green stem
waves goodbye
to winter

the end

Other books of poetry by Elliot M. Rubin

Scrambled Poems from my Heart
A Boutique Bouquet of Poems and Stories
Rumblings of an Old Man
Surf Avenue Girl - semi episodic poetry
Flash Pan Poetry
Unrequited Love
Aliyah - an Episodic Memoir
My Life if I took a Different Path -
      an Episodic Memoire
Bent Twigs and Wet Feet
Stories of the South
Selected Poems by Elliot M. Rubin
Chains of Love and other Poems
Cookies and milk with poetry

www.CreativeFiction.net

www.ingramcontent.com/pod-product-compliance
Lightning Source LLC
Chambersburg PA
CBHW060936050426
42453CB00009B/1035